Amazing Words

Edited By Allanah Jackson-James

First published in Great Britain in 2020 by:

Young Writers
Remus House
Coltsfoot Drive
Peterborough
PE2 9BF
Telephone: 01733 890066
Website: www.youngwriters.co.uk

Printed and bound in the UK by BookPrintingUK
Website: www.bookprintinguk.com
YB0442B

★ FOREWORD

Here at Young Writers our defining aim is to promote the joys of reading and writing to children and young adults and we are committed to nurturing the creative talents of the next generation. By allowing them to see their own work in print we believe their confidence and love of creative writing will grow.

Out Of This World is our latest fantastic competition, specifically designed to encourage the writing skills of primary school children through the medium of poetry. From the high quality of entries received, it is clear that it really captured the imagination of all involved.

We are proud to present the resulting collection of poems that we are sure will amuse and inspire.

An absorbing insight into the imagination and thoughts of the young, we hope you will agree that this fantastic anthology is one to delight the whole family again and again.

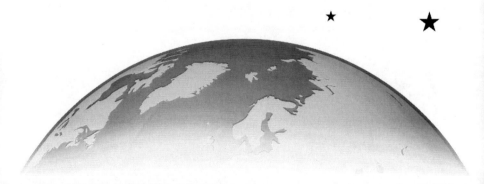

CONTENTS

Millway Primary School, Duston

Millie Johnson (9)	64
Patryk Kowalski (9)	65
Toby Stockton (8)	66
Olivia Saunders (9)	67
Ethan Verlander (9)	68
Edmund Puchovic (8)	69
Gwen Anyaeji (8)	70
Ellie McCleave (8)	71
Isla Tallett (9)	72
Max Vaughan (8)	73
Eloise Baker (9)	74
Aaliyah Hamdy (8)	75
Naomi Pinto (8)	76
Daniel Ipati (9)	77
Maisie Etheridge (8)	78
Harry Ashby (9)	79
Freyja Painting (8)	80
Laura Rzezniczak (9)	81
Keoma Brown Goddey (8)	82
Kaleb Elvy (8)	83
Francesca Cannata (8)	84
Eleanor Hemmings (8)	85
Lucas Smith (8)	86
Yunus Hussain (8)	87

Riverview Primary School, Stapenhill

Aleysha Yates (11)	88
Lucy Grubb (10)	89
Alina Spiridonova (11)	90
Dylan Titley (10)	91
Adrian Durlik (11)	92
Charlie Mayne (10)	93
Marika Makarenko (11)	94

Sacred Heart Catholic Primary School, Leeds

Huzaifa Tahir (10)	95
Kristjana Reardon (11)	96
Mirabell Nleya (11)	97

Maria Alenad (11)	98
Milly Gillon (10)	99
Carrick Njinko (11)	100
Leah Paul Bata (11)	101
Robin Brugnot (10)	102
Olivia Kennedy (11)	103
Libby Ilechie (11)	104
Joshua Mhlanga (11)	105
Tanishka Senthilkumar (10)	106
Elizabeth Young (10)	107
Shae Taiwo-Sewell (10)	108
Isla Sweeney (10)	109

St Luke's Halsall CE Primary School, Liverpool

Kessia Speers (10)	110
Camryn Williams (11)	111
Lucy Ainscough (11)	112
Lily-Mae Cureton (10)	113
Grace Critchley (11)	114
Nathan Hughes (11)	115
Austin Williams (11)	116
Grace Dawson (10)	117
Lilly Rose McParlan (11)	118
Amy Martin (11)	119
Robyn Cunningham (10)	120
Vinu Wewalwala (11)	121
Isaac Moran (10)	122
Connor Dwyer (11)	123
Shay Gorman (10)	124
Ava Hargreaves (10)	125
Lyla Durdey (10)	126
Sienna Nugent (11)	127
Edward Fell (11)	128
Rose Gartland (10)	129
Lizzie Smith (11)	130
Jessica Dearden (10)	131
Tom Windsor (11)	132
Jamie Aldridge (11)	133

St Mary's CE Primary School, Chiddingfold

Jessica Pendegrass (9)	134
Amber Talman	136
Mattie Thompson	138
Florence Spicer (10)	140
Joseph Mercer (9)	142
Lily Sabi Parry (9)	144
Lila Cooke (9)	146
Bea Monk (9)	148
Owen Wilson (9)	150
Noah McCarthy-Holland (9)	152
Edward Seymour	154
Isaac Lee-Smith (10)	155
Camille Freeman Lecerf (9)	156
Findlay Price	158
Jasmine Rollings	160
Evelyn Harrison (9)	162
Ben Church (9)	163
Samuel Ponting (10)	164
Barnaby Harrall (9)	165
Jessica Dawes (10)	166
Toby Bennett (9)	167
Max Cansfield (9)	168

THE POEMS

My Lunch Box

I open my lunch box,
What will I find?
A sandwich or wrap?
All different kinds.
Cheese, Nutella or ham,
Tomato, cucumber or jam.

I open my lunch box,
What will I find?
Some fruit or vegetables?
All different kinds.
Strawberries, salad or cherries,
Apples, pears or berries.

I open my lunch box,
What will I find?
Some chocolate or treats?
All different kinds.
KitKat, Twix or cake,
Oreo, cookies or flake.
Yummy! Yummy!
Delicious and tasty!

Penelope South (8)
Aberdare Town CIW Primary School, Aberdare

Minecraft

Majestic Minecraft is a place,
Full of building blocks,
And big, beautiful biomes.
You can kill creatures,
Find dancing diamonds,
The magical mystical meadows,
Offer a peaceful place to play.

I can build big beautiful buildings,
Or dig deep down through the dirt.
But when the light levels get too low,
The world becomes quite scary.
Creepers crawling carefully,
And spiders scuttling by.

I've got to be wary,
In a cave I create,
A colossal home of mine,
With a bed, a chest,
And a furnace by my side.

Digging for diamonds,
Is dreadfully hard,

But a chore that must be done.
They're super sparkly,
And spectacularly hard.
Great for my protection.

I wish the world,
Was more like Minecraft,
A place to laugh and play.
Where I can alter the settings,
When I choose and make it,
Permanently day!

Elijah Harris (8)
Aberdare Town CIW Primary School, Aberdare

Space And Aliens

Aliens live in super space,
And they live on an odd,
Odd planet,
Called Alien City.
Two aliens on that planet,
Are best friends,
Called Zip and Zap.
They are as green as grass,
And as clever as scientists,
And as slimy as a fish or slime.
They were also as good as God.

But two aliens,
Were best friends.
But they were as mean as a witch,
Or a wizard.
And as slimy as a fish,
And as clever as a scientist.
Their names were Glog and Cog.
They planned to destroy Mars,
Turn it into a Mars bar,
And eat it.

But Zap was fighting,
And Zip was brave,
And shot Glog and Cog,
With a laser.

Erin Taylor (8)
Aberdare Town CIW Primary School, Aberdare

My Daddy, The Rugby Referee

The day I went to Cardiff,
To watch my daddy referee,
Wales were playing the Italians,
I felt as proud as can be!

At the Principality Stadium,
The greatest of them all.
My daddy stood next to Alun Wyn Jones,
He looked ever so small!

Sixty-eight thousand, singing the anthem,
And roars from the crowd,
"Wales! Wales! Wales!"
Came the sound from all around.

A hat-trick for Adams and a try for North,
The fierce Welsh attack!
Penalties and conversions,
With a mighty strong pack!

Today we beat the Italians,
Forty-two to zero,
But I was there supporting,
My daddy and my hero!

Parker Morris (8)
Aberdare Town CIW Primary School, Aberdare

I Love Chocolate

If chocolate was a feeling,
It would be the happiest feeling of all.
If chocolate was a mountain,
It would be Mount Everest!
If chocolate was a person,
It would be my BFF.
If chocolate was a hobby,
It would be like riding a fast bike.
If chocolate was an animal,
It would be a cute puppy.
If chocolate was a holiday,
It would be Disney World.
If chocolate was a time of year,
It would be October.
I love chocolate,
Do you love it too?

Molly Matthews (8)
Aberdare Town CIW Primary School, Aberdare

Awful Aliens

Some aliens crashed into town,
And everyone there had a frown.
But the aliens said with a smile,
"We've come further than a mile."
Please wipe those frowns from off your face,
We all live in a place called 'space'.
We have flown from that far star,
To try a delicious chocolate bar,
And we little green men,
Are keen to see Big Ben.
In our pockets,
We have toy rockets.
Do you fancy a race,
Into outer space?

Mali Hawker (8)
Aberdare Town CIW Primary School, Aberdare

Polar Bears

P eople love polar bears.
O nce I saw a polar bear.
L eaving his igloo.
A nd he was playing in the snow.
R eally, polar bears are nice.

B ears eat fish.
E veryone is scared of polar bears but not me!
A polar bear lives in the attic.
R emember, polar bears run fast!
S o look out if you see one coming.

Ella Prosser (8)
Aberdare Town CIW Primary School, Aberdare

Games Are What I Like To Do

Games, games,
Begin with G.
PlayStation and Xbox,
Are the consoles for me.

With my controller,
I have the power,
Power to run, jump,
Dodge and ground pound,
Like a superpower.

Look at the screen,
And let the games begin.
Please be kind like me,
And don't play games,
That will hurt your mind,
And give you nightmares.

Travis Walsh (8)
Aberdare Town CIW Primary School, Aberdare

Good Morning Spring

Spring has woken,
Her hands touch the sky.
She softly whispers sweet words,
To the early birds as they fly.

She rolls along the lush green grass,
And plays amongst the bees.
Shhh... listen closely,
You can hear her laughing with the trees.

Beautiful spring is here,
Warm and wonderful and bright.
Spring good morning,
Winter goodnight.

Ruby Driscoll (8)
Aberdare Town CIW Primary School, Aberdare

Indescribable Voyage Out Of This World!

What was it like,
On that first flight,
To see the Earth from above?
Five,
Four,
Three,
Two,
One,
Blast-off!
This was a historic moment,
That nobody thought would happen.
Did the astronaut open his eyes,
To gaze upon the spectre of the universe?
What a magnificent sight.
He saw planets, stars,
The Milky Way and Mars.

Rosanna Page (8)
Aberdare Town CIW Primary School, Aberdare

Lonely Dogs

Sometimes dogs are strays,
Some people say, "Stay."
Some dogs run away,
Sometimes dogs are whiny,
Sometimes they are tiny.
Whatever they are,
They're funny.
Please, just love each pup,
Even when they are grown up.
Don't leave them all alone.
Even when they've grown.

Esme Grace Burford (8)
Aberdare Town CIW Primary School, Aberdare

Meanings Of Justice

J ustice means fair and not fair.

U nited as one.

S ometimes things are not fair and they should be.

T hings are sometimes not fair.

I nvolves everyone.

C ares about others.

E verything should be fair.

Lily May (8)

Aberdare Town CIW Primary School, Aberdare

Holiday

H ot and sunny day.

O reo ice cream on holiday.

L ollipops all the time.

I ce cream is the best on holiday.

D ive into the pool.

A s hot as the fierce flames.

Y ay for holidays!

McKenzie Lewis (8)

Aberdare Town CIW Primary School, Aberdare

Roblox Fun

Roblox is my favourite game,
Although my mother says it's lame.
I can play alone or with my friends,
It is endless fun until it ends.
I would play all the time,
If there was no such thing as bedtime.

Noah Burford (8)
Aberdare Town CIW Primary School, Aberdare

Animals

Penguins, pandas,
Polar bears are cute.
Squirrels are lovely,
But spiders, *eew!*
Gorillas, caterpillars,
Also cheeky chimpanzees.
Unicorns are my favourite,
And so are puppies.

Lowri Davies (8)
Aberdare Town CIW Primary School, Aberdare

The Loneliest Star

S hining stars are pretty.

T hough some are lonely.

A nd very high up.

R eady to twinkle.

S o do not worry little star because I love you.

Olivia Miles (8)

Aberdare Town CIW Primary School, Aberdare

Teddies

Teddies, teddies,
So many but only one,
Is my special one.
Great big eyes,
And fluffy, white fur.
Billy is his name,
My special, favourite
Teddy bear.

Daniel Cross (8)
Aberdare Town CIW Primary School, Aberdare

Dancing Is The Best

D azzling.

A mazing.

N ice and inspiring.

C ertificate always helps.

E mbarrassing but it is always worth it.

Lexi Wilkins (8)
Aberdare Town CIW Primary School, Aberdare

Galactic Stars

Black is the colour of the universe.
Black is the colour of the solar eclipse.
Black is the colour of the night sky.

White is the colour of the stars.
White is the colour of the ice around Jupiter's ring
White is the colour of swirls on Venus.

Blue is the colour of Uranus.
Blue is the colour of Neptune.
Blue is the colour of Earth.

Yellow is the colour of the sun.
Yellow is the colour of Venus.
Yellow is the colour of Jupiter.

Jaiya Goodman
Bures CE (VC) Primary School, Bures

Space/Mars

S tars shining in the dark sky.
P luto the dwarf planet.
A ll the planets gleaming, saying hi.
C ircling the sun, the aliens are having fun.
E arth is where we live but might not be.

M agically in space.
A lways there, floating.
R eminding me of the chocolate.
S tars surrounding it.

Ruben Cook (9)

Bures CE (VC) Primary School, Bures

Senses Of Space

In space,
I can see planets,
Spinning slowly.
I can hear,
The spaceship's engine,
Rumbling.
I can smell cheese,
From the moon.
I can taste cheese,
From the moon.
I can touch the rock,
From the moon.

Cody Woodman (9)
Bures CE (VC) Primary School, Bures

Space

S aturn is dark brown and the sixth planet in the solar system.

P luto, the dwarf planet orbiting.

A wesome solar system.

C omets crashing into each other.

E arth is the only planet with life on it.

Henry Richold (10)

Bures CE (VC) Primary School, Bures

Space

S tars are shining, I am rhyming.

P luto is cool and very small.

A ll the planets are above me but I cannot see.

C ircling the sun, aliens having fun.

E arth we are living on but soon may not be.

James Bryant (10)

Bures CE (VC) Primary School, Bures

Riddle In Space

This planet was named after the Roman god of messengers.
This planet has no moons
Its colour is grey.
It is made of iron and rock
It was discovered by astronomers.
What planet is it?

Answer: Mercury.

Chloe Leith (9)
Bures CE (VC) Primary School, Bures

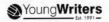

I Love Saturn

I can see the long thing,
Surrounding Saturn.
I can hear Saturn's moons,
Crashing into each other.
I can touch the freezing cold surface,
I can smell the strong gas.
I can taste the asteroid belt.

Leo Fauche (10)
Bures CE (VC) Primary School, Bures

In The Night Sky

Stunning stars in the night sky,
Shimmering planets in the night sky,
Spinning around in the night sky,
Soothing solar system in the night sky,
Spooky spotlight in the night sky.

Poppy Ames (9)
Bures CE (VC) Primary School, Bures

Space

S pinning planets.
P luto the dwarf planet.
A star is very hot.
C old space.
E ight planets in the solar system.

Oliver Richold (10)
Bures CE (VC) Primary School, Bures

Space

S olar system.
P lanets moving.
A stronauts exploring.
C ollisions happening.
E clipses beginning.

Beatrice Hart (10)
Bures CE (VC) Primary School, Bures

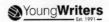

Space

S aturn, a huge gas giant
P luto, a tiny dwarf planet
A cting
C razy
E xtraordinary.

Daniel Gallier-Trigg (10)

Bures CE (VC) Primary School, Bures

Solar System And Planets

In the solar system are eight planets.
The first planet in the solar system is Mercury,
Which is rocky.
The second planet in the solar system is Venus,
Which is the hottest after the sun.
The third planet in the solar system is Earth,
Whose life begun.
The fourth planet in the solar system is Mars,
Where the weather is very harsh.
The fifth planet in the solar system is Jupiter,
Which is brown in colour.
The sixth planet in the solar system is Saturn,
Which ring shines like a laser.
The seventh planet in the solar system is Uranus,
Which you refer to as blue in colour.
The eighth planet in the solar system is Neptune,
Which is said to be the last of all.

Dhruv Vinodkumar (9)

Catherine Junior School, Leicester

Galactic Dreams

I'm a ten-year-old girl,
Who always gets distracted,
By my wonderful pen,
Which is extremely galactic.
My friends always visit at night,
Never day.
To give me a treat,
In a special way.
They always take me to space,
Then give me a toy.
Which always leads me,
To such delightful joy.
Once again tonight,
I will play amongst the stars,
To let myself see,
What spring is like on Mars.
I will then see what toys,
They will give to me today.
But when I wake to see they aren't here,
I won't be shouting yay.

One day I hope for a space helmet,
To travel to the moon.
Just so my long legs,
Can plummet there soon.
My mind is like a goldfish,
When I'm at school,
Always thinking about spaceships,
And how to be cool.
Maybe one day,
I will know I can stay up there,
Then I'll be with the astronauts,
And it'll all be fair.

Harjoth Kaur (11)
Catherine Junior School, Leicester

The Planets

There are eight planets,
In our solar system.
If you don't know them,
Then you're in luck!
Because after this,
You won't be as stuck!

First comes Mercury,
Which you learnt about in nursery.
Number two is Venus,
Which has a small weakness.
Then comes Earth,
An obsession in Perth.
After that comes Mars,
Which kind of rhymes with bars.
Then Jupiter arrives,
Which is number five.

After that comes Saturn,
Which has a unique pattern.
Next, it's Uranus,
That isn't really famous.

Finally, Neptune,
The furthest planet away,
Hooray!

Now with all these words I've used,
You won't be as confused!
Because you'll remember them,
From your head to your shoes!

Reyna Dewshi (10)
Catherine Junior School, Leicester

Space

Space is large,
Like the Milky Way afar
Planets are huge,
Like Jupiter and Neptune.

Astronauts sometimes,
Are a bit scared.
Because when they walk in space,
They will go nowhere.
But at the same time,
They are quite excited.
Because when they go,
They and space are united.

There are four rocky planets;
On them,
You can see the stars.
Mercury,
Venus,
Earth and Mars.
There are four gas giants;

They're more than 100,000 kilometres,
Away from us.
Saturn,
Uranus,
Neptune,
And the biggest one,
Jupiter.

There are also moons,
Everyone's assured.
Jupiter has the most.
It has sixty-three moons!

Kashvi Camal (10)
Catherine Junior School, Leicester

Dive Into Space

Out of the world,
We go and see some dazzling,
Spectacular things.
Stars, planets, galaxies,
Just waiting to be seen.
They might be big or tiny,
But beautiful in life.
To go to space,
You will need a rocket,
To fly high,
High and high.
But when you look up,
In the sky at night,
Have you ever wondered,
What's out there?
What's beyond the solar system,
Far into the distance.
The universe is very big,
Bigger than everything,
You can possibly imagine.
But the empty space between,

In fact, is everything that exists.
One moment there was nothing,
But all of a sudden,
Bang!
Life happened.
It was called the Big Bang.

Poojitha Gunapanedu (9)
Catherine Junior School, Leicester

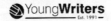

Planet To Planet

I blast from Earth and land on the moon
I collect moon rocks and soon head to Venus
Venus is too hot
Planet to planet, all day long
I land on Mercury, it's too close to the sun
Ouch! It's burning me to death!
Soon I reach Mars, I see humongous volcanoes
about to erupt
Planet to planet and now it's Jupiter, wow!
It's super-duper big!
Now I reach my dream planet, I see an icy ring
I could skate on it but it is made of glass!
Planet to planet, I land on Uranus
I find out it's the coldest
At last, I reach Neptune
Oh, it's so very far!
I am really tired, I want to go back to Earth
Planet to planet all day long!

Siya Bhatt (7)
Catherine Junior School, Leicester

Areas Of Space

Space, space,
How wonderful,
How beautiful.
The solar system is glorious,
And magical.
Galaxies are so starry and shiny,
The view is like a magical star,
It's as shiny as a shiny card.
No one can resist the view,
It's very nice and out of the world,
No matter how dark or how bright,
Just the way I like it.
In every different way if you meet it,
You will think it's the best place ever.
Brings good memories to me.
Space is one of the best memories,
I had in my entire life.
You think it's nothing,
But to me, it's a dream come true.

Sriya Manilal (7)
Catherine Junior School, Leicester

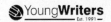

My Little Star Called Neptune

Neptune, Neptune,
You're so high in the sky
Neptune, Neptune,
You're a wonder up in the sky,
Maybe we could ponder why you are so far.

But please,
Just wait.
Don't get icy or afraid.
We're here to help you,
And give you some aid.

Maybe we can help you,
Like the stars before,
And make you less icy and less cold.

It looks like a little gas ball,
High up in the sky.
Maybe it is a star,
Or just a little fly.

But you look so bright,
Almost as if you were a little firefly.
Floating in the dark night sky.
Every star has a story,
And this story is mine!

Isra Said (10)
Catherine Junior School, Leicester

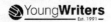

My Friends

Friends that are always happy,
Supportive when there is no one.
Friends help us with anything,
At any time.
They always care for each other.

Friends always make you smile,
When you are sad.
They tell you jokes to keep you happy.

Friends never judge,
They don't care,
What country you are from,
And what religion you follow.

They are always there to support you,
And keep you happy!
Friends are like brothers.
They love you as much as your brother.
I love my friends.

Jenilkumar Manoj (7)
Catherine Junior School, Leicester

Five Little Astronauts

Five little astronauts,
Flying in the stars.
The first one said,
"Let's go see Mars!"
The second one said,
"There are comets in the air!"
The third one said,
"There is an alien here!"
The fourth one said,
"Let's fly up in the sky!"
The fifth one said,
"Let's go really high!"
Then *whoosh!*
Went the spaceship.
Buckle up tight!
And the five astronauts,
Zoomed out of sight.

Elda Dound (9)
Catherine Junior School, Leicester

Shooting Star!

S ee that flying across the sky.
H igher than the moon.
O ut in space it twinkles.
O ver the clouds and dust.
T winkling like a jewel.
I t speeds through the night.
N ever stops for anyone.
G lowing in the dark.

S himmering, shooting stars.
T hat shines a bright gold.
A nd glitters with a sparkle.
R ushing through the night!

Jinal Sheth (9)
Catherine Junior School, Leicester

Star Of The Week

I'm a star and I play a game,
I don't always look the same.

Sometimes I'm bright,
Like a light.

Sometimes I'm pointy,
Like a sharp knife.

Sometimes I surprise you,
Then hide for a while.

Sometimes I shine,
As bright as a diamond.

Look up in the sky,
For my friendly light.

What shape will I be
When you see me tonight?

Imogen Simpson (9)
Catherine Junior School, Leicester

Going To The Moon

Soon I was going to the moon,
With a balloon till noon.
When we went to Mars,
We saw nearby stars.
They were shaped,
Like chocolate bars!
When we arrived we saw aliens,
They were making a stadium,
They also had uranium,
That was bigger than the titanium!
Then I realised that my shoes,
Were the colour of blue,
And it was stuck with glue!
How could I do this
Without you?

Siddhanth Mayur (10)
Catherine Junior School, Leicester

NASA Space

I'll gather up these shooting stars,
That cascade across my cheeks.
Ill-fated sentiments and desires expelled,
To alleviate the pressure my heart is under.

I'll dash them across the sky,
To create another incandescent constellation,
To admire.
Another fable to recognise,
Another myth to romanticise,
And another light to help,
Guide me through the night.

Dharmik Patel (10)
Catherine Junior School, Leicester

Planet Poem

Mercury is the closest planet to the sun.
Venus comes next, it is the hottest one.
Eath comes third,
The only life we know.
Mars has the largest canyon and volcano!
The gassy planet Jupiter,
The largest you will find.
Saturn has rings around the outside.
Uranus is funny...
'Cause he spins on his side.
Neptune looks blue,
The coolest of its kind.

Vishwjeet Gill (7)

Catherine Junior School, Leicester

Oh Moon!

Silvery moon!
I see your face high in the sky,
That is your place.
When the sun sets,
You appear.
In the darkest of night,
When nobody is there

Oh moon!
Oh silvery moon!
Sometimes it is a crest.
Sometimes it is a full moon.

On the moon,
Little astronauts fly.
Like little stars,
Shimmering in the sky.

Zunairah Patel (8)
Catherine Junior School, Leicester

My Space Dream

Twelve o'clock at midnight,
I had a dream.
A dream of space,
I went in a space shuttle.
To travel around space world.

There was a lot of planets,
In different, different sizes.

I saw numerous stars,
Gleaming through the dark sky.

Then my space shuttle went boom!
And I woke up with a zoom!

Darsh Vaghela (7)
Catherine Junior School, Leicester

The Beautiful Space

The beautiful space is dark,
The beautiful space is bright.
The beautiful space is scary.
The beautiful space is delightful.
Do you think space is good?
Do you think space is bad?
Is space dark?
Is space bright?
Sun,
Venus,
Mercury,
Earth,
Jupiter,
Saturn,
Neptune and Mars.

Sahibpreet Singh (9)
Catherine Junior School, Leicester

Wonderful Planets And Shiny Stars

What wonderful planets!
They are so colourful.
Bright stars in the night sky,
So many twinkling stars too.
There are lots of different types of planets,
Pluto is a dwarf planet.
Colourful planets in the space.
We live on Earth,
Earth is such a clean and beautiful planet.
Such a nice place!

Jiya Patel (8)

Catherine Junior School, Leicester

The Solar System

Far, far in the sky,
I see a world of space.
Where the stars always gleam,
And the moon sheens.

The galaxy with more,
Than twenty billion suns,
Is the light it gives,
Shining oh so brightly,
In a sky that lives.
The solar system with eight planets,
Shimmers in the night sky.

Eesha Vaghela (10)
Catherine Junior School, Leicester

To The Moon

Climb up to the rocket,
Here we go.
Hurry up the rocket,
Gonna blast-off!

Put on your helmet,
And buckle up.
Ten, nine, eight,
Seven, six, five,
Four, three, two,
One,
Blast-off!

Heet Baria (8)
Catherine Junior School, Leicester

My Adventure

Minkey the cheeky monkey was swinging in a tree
when he saw a bee
Suddenly the bee started buzzing at the tree
As night fell, this story I began to tell
Of a robber who had a dog called Dodder that was
a hogger
We all huddled together and we started to cuddle
As it got as dark as the colour black
In the morning, we were yawning
We went to school and went into the hall and leant
against the wall
At the end of the day, we went home a different
way.

Isla Barville (7)

Fir Tree Primary School & Nursery, Newbury

Me And Two Dogs!

Once I saw two dogs
And they hugged some frogs
My brothers and me, I am Riley
Then saw my girlfriend Kiley

Me and my dogs saw a cat
And it was wearing a big woolly hat

Then it was getting dark
So the dogs started to bark
Then we started to sleep
And there was a beep

Then it was morning
Outside there was a warning
We went to hockey
And we saw a person called Rocky

We then went to the jungle
And we saw my uncle
Scooby was kissing
And he went missing

We opened the door
And saw a muddy paw
We saw a cat
Racing a grumpy rat.

Riley John Cotter (7)
Fir Tree Primary School & Nursery, Newbury

The Naughty Cat

We were in the living room watching TV when we heard a noise upstairs. We all went up and there was a black cat named Whoopie. It hissed and scratched and we screamed, "Argh!" We all ran away.
Whoopie was on our bed licking her paws then she got as spoiled as the Queen. Then we all said hello to her and she purred.

Lola Holmes (8)
Fir Tree Primary School & Nursery, Newbury

The Power Cut

Me and my little sister and my mummy went to the park. I cheerfully said, "Yay, we can have a cupcake!" Then we went back home and there was a humongous grey cloud, it was thundering. The electric went off and the power went off also so then we played some games until it was over.

Dylan Knight (7)
Fir Tree Primary School & Nursery, Newbury

Space

The majestic twilight stars put on a show whilst I gaze up above.
Gently, the galaxy twinkles in the new world.
Abruptly the planet moves, orbiting the Earth.
A twinkle of stardust gently dances on my cheek.

Catastrophically the planets hit my feelings.
Mars' redness in my heart.
Neptune's blue in my eyes.
And a vast stardust twinkles in my smile.

All colours warm me and welcome me at home.
As I lay in the cosmos, stars and more.
The Earth's twinkling lights shoot into space like a ball.
Space is beautiful, I hope you come too.

Millie Johnson (9)
Millway Primary School, Duston

Space

A solid planet flies majestically.
The rocky moon creps silently.
The strong planets fight lifelessly.
The only planet with life stands out from them all.

A vast amount of stars are dancers.
We are just a speck of the universe.
All of the unknown we shall not see.
We're looking for life signs, what if there is none at all?

I hang from the stars.
A meteoroid is coming for me.
A vast amount of galaxies fighting for their land.
Some gigantic stars weakly shining.

Patryk Kowalski (9)
Millway Primary School, Duston

The Space Poem

The bright colours dance slowly in the distance.
A huge planet rotates slowly in the stary night.
The round moon stays still,
Silently sending white reflections wherever it goes.
The shiny stars looked down at the people quietly,
Reminding the people of their family members.
The gigantic rocket ships moving loudly,
From different directions of the galaxy.
An invisible gravity lifted people up gently to the stars,
The little shooting stars ran quickly around the brightness.

Toby Stockton (8)
Millway Primary School, Duston

Space

Iridescently, the glistening galaxy shines majestically.
The scattered stars are filled with happiness.
A colourful spaceship dodged sophisticated and beautiful planets.
Majestically, one planet is lit up by the moon.

The twilight stardust spreads softly like butter.
An angry fireball makes an entrance unhappily.
Silently, the peaceful Earth swirls around the whole of the unknown.
The plain moon brings the dark out to come and play.

Olivia Saunders (9)
Millway Primary School, Duston

Out Of This World

The startled galaxy stormed destructively.
One glamorous star danced like no one was watching.
Saturn's ring circled around me like a hula-hoop.

A balmy fireball discharges angrily.
In the void of space, one lonely star waits silently.
Neptune's blue awakens my eyes shining like the sun.

Majestically, the unhappy planets burn near the sun.
Staring at the sun, my pupils burst.
The vague sun slowly pivots around.

Ethan Verlander (9)
Millway Primary School, Duston

Space

The shining stars floated wonderfully in the midnight sky.
Silently, the majestic colours decorated outer space.
The rocket planets twirled slowly in the dark space.
The dangerous meteoroids darted rapidly to Earth.

The solid rocket landed carefully on the moon.
A shooting star flew silently past Earth.
An inky black hole twirled nervously while covering the stars.
The twinkling stardust shines beautifully next to giant planets.

Edmund Puchovic (8)

Millway Primary School, Duston

The Galaxy

The astonishing stardust circled silently.
A colourful galaxy swirled towards the solar
system.
Silently, the beautiful planet surrounded and ran
around the sun.
A graceful skyline kissed the stars.
The stunning stars floated around the sun.

The magnificent meteor burned towards the Earth.
A spectacular spaceship flew through space.
The solar system danced around the sky.
A ring of Saturn flew around her like a hula-hoop.

Gwen Anyaeji (8)
Millway Primary School, Duston

Space Life

The twilight stars consumed the startling moon.
An indigo shine caught the glow of my eye.
The mixed, multicoloured skyline made my cheeks shimmer.
The majestic stardust hovered across me.
The Milky Way retreated towards me like a lightning bolt.
As the spaceships glided around the transparent air swiftly.
The frequent moon chuckled all over.
Round Saturn, rings fit around me.
A gentle chaos galaxy moved perfectly like clouds.

Ellie McCleave (8)
Millway Primary School, Duston

Space Wonders!

The rocky planet twirled speechlessly.
A bright star shot across the sky magically.
The colourful galaxy night sat silently.
As the glinting night sky spread along the night.

All the stars sparkling with brightness.
As the stars were hovering over the amazing Earth.
The powerful sky made my feelings burst.
Could the amazing planets really be real with their amazingness?

Isla Tallett (9)
Millway Primary School, Duston

Outer Space

The dangerous planet spins slowly.
A beautiful wormhole takes you to the unknown.
An amazing star shoots gently.
The fascinating ring moves with Saturn.

The vast galaxy opens a fresh wormhole.
A hard meteoroid takes on the Earth.
The dark moon covers the sun to make it visible.
An adventurous rocket dives into outer space.

Max Vaughan (8)
Millway Primary School, Duston

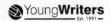

What Is Space?

Yellow paint splodges everywhere.
An endless room of emptiness.
People flying all around the place.
The unbreathable atmosphere of the galaxy.
Planets having a hula-hoop competition.

Planets jealous of Earth.
Black hole killer machine.
Sprinkles of stardust on my cheek.
Rock like gun bullets.
Never-ending falls.

Eloise Baker (9)
Millway Primary School, Duston

The Galaxy

A smooth planet dancing peacefully.
A dreaming planet twirls.
The cold air blows swiftly.
The bright veil of colours fills the air.

A shiny star is bright like the sun.
The soft moon is transparent as ever.
A beautiful star stands out from the crowd.
The wonders of space hide its true features.

Aaliyah Hamdy (8)
Millway Primary School, Duston

You Are Like The Stars In Space!

Splashed planets giggle in their wake.
Gloomy galaxies spread apart as they zoom across the universe.
Scattered stars shine up above as they chat to their friends.
Glowing voids greedily swallow up the galaxy like a black hole.
Midnight moon searches the galaxy, ready for an adventure!

Naomi Pinto (8)
Millway Primary School, Duston

The Empire Of Planets

Expanding cosmos never stops for some reason.
Open space protects the beautiful Earth from the burning hot meteors.
Vast planets get excited as it's their birthdays.
Splashes of colour fill the hollow void.
Infinite stars smile with sadness during their life in the galaxy.

Daniel Ipati (9)

Millway Primary School, Duston

Our Outer Space!

Cantankerous clouds rage like a bull.
Splashes of colour fill the hollow air void.
Infinite stars lay proudly and fill our outer space.
Our blinding moon disintegrates as life passes by.
A million pinpricks of planets frown with loneliness.

Maisie Etheridge (8)
Millway Primary School, Duston

Space

I wish I could lie in a dream amongst the galaxy.
The cosmos staring at you like a bull.
Galaxies spread like a rainbow.
The moon was blinding.
Infinite space stands like the Statue of Liberty.
Stars glow sadly, waiting for a friend.

Harry Ashby (9)
Millway Primary School, Duston

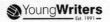

Twittering Space

Swirling whirlpools spread across the galaxy.
Dazzling Earth turns gradually.
Our midnight moon reflects off the infinite sun.
Explosions of stars spin across the cosmos.
Sprinting comets explode planets across the
mysterious space.

Freyja Painting (8)
Millway Primary School, Duston

Space

Illuminating stars sparkle until daylight ends.
Splashes of colours fill the hollow void.
The lonely moon sits while watching other planets laughing.
Flashing galaxies stand there all alone.
Suspended planets smile sadly at Earth.

Laura Rzezniczak (9)
Millway Primary School, Duston

Space As Deep As Secrets

Colossal planets look down sadly at Earth.
Twinkling stars spread themselves out at night.
Splashes of colour fill the sky.
Infinite cosmos stare down at astronauts.
Expanding galaxies are waiting impatiently to be found.

Keoma Brown Goddey (8)

Millway Primary School, Duston

Intergalactic Space

Cantankerous planets stare in anger.
Open stars enter the void.
True colours spread, bringing joy to all of the
empires.
A levitating man sprints around the galaxy,
groaning for help.
Ever growing cosmos makes jaws drop.

Kaleb Elvy (8)
Millway Primary School, Duston

The Open Wonder

Saturn's rings encompass planets.
Empty-handed stars cry and race down to nothing.
Splashes of colour fight through the darkness.
Infinite cosmos hugs the galaxies.
Jupiter's storm rages like a bull.

Francesca Cannata (8)
Millway Primary School, Duston

Space

Colourful galaxies move around me.
Golden asteroids fall behind me.
Transparent satellite beams try to find me.
A miniature Earth surrounded by the void that I lie in.
Scattered rocks surround me.

Eleanor Hemmings (8)

Millway Primary School, Duston

What Happens In Space!

Galaxy colours splash into the hollow void.
Stardust like atoms spread on your cheek like
freckles.
Darkness invites the planets to shine.
A dimpled moon gradually consumes the void in
space.

Lucas Smith (8)
Millway Primary School, Duston

Galaxy

An exploration of supernovas,
Stealing the colours.
The excellent cosmos waiting to be explored.
A dimpled moon shining down at the Earth.
Yellow stars showing the way to other planets.

Yunus Hussain (8)
Millway Primary School, Duston

Going Through Space

Going through space
Is really super ace.
Orbiting the planets
While eating pomegranates.
Going past the moon and a star,
Shouting loudly, au revoir!
Then I see an alien,
Turns out he's Romanian.
He hops down to his friends,
So his friendship with them will never end.
Alien teachers teach
And asks the pupils a question each.
The teacher talks about poets
And soon everyone wants to know it.
Going through space
Is really super ace
But not with an alien on your case!

Aleysha Yates (11)
Riverview Primary School, Stapenhill

Zooming Through Space

Zooming through space
Is really, really nice.
Going past the moon and a star,
Shouting loudly, au revoir!

Very fast space cars speed on by,
We cruise along like a butterfly.
While we orbit the planet
We satisfy ourselves by eating a pomegranate.

Space teachers stand and teach,
Whilst eating a lovely peach.
The class gets quickly bored,
Some of them snored.
Then the teacher talks about poets,
Suddenly, everyone wants to know it.

Lucy Grubb (10)
Riverview Primary School, Stapenhill

Space

Space,
It is truly a beautiful place,
Totally not a disgrace,
Actually, it is full of grace!

I then spot an alien named Drace,
He isn't like my friend Grace.
Drace then said,
"Come to our place,
We have a lot of alien race!"

When I go to see their place,
I have to tie my shoelace.
It feels like a disgrace
So I go to the maze.

Alina Spiridonova (11)
Riverview Primary School, Stapenhill

Space At Night

I look at space at night,
The stars are very bright.
They go quickly out of sight,
Travelling at the speed of light.

I look at space at night,
There are lots of meteorites,
It is the best at midnight,
The stars are set alight.

I look at space at night.
The moon is a searchlight.
It's also a campsite,
For stars that are in flight.

Dylan Titley (10)
Riverview Primary School, Stapenhill

Space

Space,
What a wonderful place
And not a disgrace,
Unlike Grace.
Now grab your suitcase,
Just in case.

I see an alien,
His name is Ace.
He likes to race,
He does the sock race.

I can play the bass,
While I go down the staircase,
And look at the showcase
In the star's workplace,
Also known as space.

Adrian Durlik (11)
Riverview Primary School, Stapenhill

Space!

Space
Is a very good place.
Space
Is a very nice place.
Is not a disgrace,
Unlike my friend Grace.

Space,
It is time to tie your shoelace
While I play my bass.

Space,
There are aliens that like to race,
So we try to chase
But we never catch up.

Charlie Mayne (10)
Riverview Primary School, Stapenhill

Space The Ace

I love looking at space.
I watch it in a place.
It is the case,
Because I am the ace.

I love watching the stars,
In my mum's car.
I eat a bar
In a space car.

Marika Makarenko (11)
Riverview Primary School, Stapenhill

The Snake Of Death!

This snake is not like any other snake
But it's the deadliest snake yet
Known as the rapid killer but crowned
As king of the jungle
It comes out at night to fight
As long as a train
And thick as a fully grown man
It kills to fill its mouth
All thanks to its razor-sharp, bloody fangs
It crawls and drools towards its food
It kills rabbits in its burrow
What sorrow
Animals say his 'fame is lame'
And 'when he's mad, he's bad'
He is lonely as possible
His venom is worse than ever
You would never want to go near him.

Huzaifa Tahir (10)
Sacred Heart Catholic Primary School, Leeds

Sentenced Seasons

Leaves are falling, the trees get boring
The pumpkins are lit, go get the glow sticks
Be careful now, for snow comes around
But a Christmas goal is winter snow
Presents are opened, it could be a bike
Or equipment to hike!
Christmas is done, spring will go on
Going back to school makes me feel blue
Now flowers are born, even roses with thorns
And trees grow green like summer has only seen
On my new bike, I'll do what I like
I've had some fun, now I will relax in the sun.

Kristjana Reardon (11)
Sacred Heart Catholic Primary School, Leeds

Ten Years Today With Climate Change

Ten years today, our world won't be safe
All because of climate change
Pollution here, pollution there
All around our polluted air
Animals die, animals suffer
All because of the terrible weather
Ten years today, the world will be in
Its worst possible state
All because of climate change
Greta Thunberg has spoken the truth
Now we have something to do
Ten years today, what did we do?
Plastic is not our worst fear
Climate change is doomed.

Mirabell Nleya (11)
Sacred Heart Catholic Primary School, Leeds

Blue Winter

I was built here,
No one really comes here.
There is a bunch of snow,
I don't really know.
Why is the snow on my head?
I should go head to bed.
I am so cold,
I feel bold.
I wake up next morning,
It is boring.
My body is bare,
I have nothing to wear.
Reindeer are flying,
I am crying.
Christmas is coming,
Elves are running.
I feel proud,
Christmas is loud.
I make cookies
For the bullies.

Maria Alenad (11)
Sacred Heart Catholic Primary School, Leeds

Family Are Funny, Friends Are Nice

My favourite colour is purple
My sister has a turtle
My mum is so cool
She likes to chill in the pool
My dad makes me laugh every day
Then he says, "Hey!"
My BFF, Olivia, is so nice
And I like ice!
Tanishka is so funny
Lexi had a bunny
My grandma is so lovely
Her dog isn't so woolly
Grandad is so smart
His favourite food is a tart
My other grandma is so kind
She has never been fined!

Milly Gillon (10)
Sacred Heart Catholic Primary School, Leeds

Bright Future

When I grow up, I could fly to the sky,
Do what I want, my life will be mine.
I'm the hero of my kind, no more class, that's what
I like.
Time is going, got to fulfil my dream fast.
Football is my current option, flying in the sky is
one of my options too.
Fulfilling my dreams will be my biggest
achievement,
Joining a Premier League club will be my biggest
achievement.
I hope you like my poem, my future will be glowing.

Carrick Njinko (11)
Sacred Heart Catholic Primary School, Leeds

Springing Sun

Leaves are growing
The wind is flowing
All in the springing sun

The birds are tweeting
The herds aren't sleeping
All in the springing sun

People are jogging
The branches are flogging
All in the springing sun

Space is walking
The planets are shaking
All in the springing sun

This is the spring, the nicest thing
Through the nice springing sun.

Leah Paul Bata (11)
Sacred Heart Catholic Primary School, Leeds

The Earth

The Earth is one of the most beautiful planets
The Earth is covered with ice, oceans and forests
But it will only stay that way if you help preserve it
Bush fires, deforestation and climate change
Are all threatening the planet
So when you leave your home
Be sure to turn off the heater
Or else the Earth will die a slow, painful death
Because of us.

Robin Brugnot (10)
Sacred Heart Catholic Primary School, Leeds

Elizabella's Poem

Elizabella has a brother.
Huck has a lover.
Elizabella has a huge, fluffy knot.
She tries to make dinner in a pot.
Minnie is the biggest prankster.
Toddyberry is a cool dancer.
Everyone hates Lemony Pinch.
Miss Duck does a flinch.
Eva and Ava love history.
Elizabella loves to find a mystery.
Minnie is really cool.
Huck loves school.

Olivia Kennedy (11)
Sacred Heart Catholic Primary School, Leeds

The Special Idol

My hero is Robin Stevens
Who inspires me like a star
It makes me create imagination
Which is definitely hard
If I can carry on in the future
I will be creative
To show my drawing skills
I won't be suspected
Giving my happiness
I would lend it to you
To show my iconic pictures
This is totally true.

Libby Ilechie (11)
Sacred Heart Catholic Primary School, Leeds

Josh's Poem

Cheetahs are running and people are clapping.
Cheetahs are running and people are crying.
Cheetahs are running like the Flash,
And people are running in a dash.
Cheetahs roar and people shout.
Cheetahs leap as high as they can,
And people jump as high as they can.
Cheetahs are vicious and people are terrified.

Joshua Mhlanga (11)
Sacred Heart Catholic Primary School, Leeds

Spring Is Here

Flowers are blooming
Spring is looming
The season of cold is far away
No snow on the ground for another day
Beautiful birds come out of their nests
After a nice, calming rest
Go out and have some fun
Then relax with a nice bun
After all, spring is here
It's the season of fun and cheer.

Tanishka Senthilkumar (10)
Sacred Heart Catholic Primary School, Leeds

Secrets Of Winter

Layers and layers
Of gleaming snow
Falls down around me
While the wind blows
Why did winter come on this day?
All those secrets are hidden away
Now that winter's coming to an end
Next is spring on its way
Time is being wasted away
That is all I have to say.

Elizabeth Young (10)
Sacred Heart Catholic Primary School, Leeds

Superheroes And Monsters

Comic books are funny,
They make me feel sunny.
Monsters make me scared,
I better get prepared.
The pictures will show
What the monsters might know.
Superheroes come out,
They fight the monsters without a doubt.
The goodies have won,
The baddies are done.

Shae Taiwo-Sewell (10)
Sacred Heart Catholic Primary School, Leeds

Layla's Rocket Ship...

Layla is going on her favourite rocket ship.
She's going into space on a trip.
She's going to Mars,
To get a bigger vase.
When she gets there,
She's going to surf in the air,
Just like she doesn't care!

Isla Sweeney (10)
Sacred Heart Catholic Primary School, Leeds

Choices And Consequences

Choices and consequences,
Affect family and friends just by holding a knife or bullet.
Murdering, unpleasant, mistakes.
Like a pack of wolves surrounding you
And staring at you with menacing eyes.
Like an extremely hungry cat chasing innocent mice.
It makes me feel worried and terrified inside.
Like having a nightmare that keeps coming back every night.
Regrets that will haunt you forever.

Kessia Speers (10)

St Luke's Halsall CE Primary School, Liverpool

Troublemakers

Troublemakers,
All they cause is chaos.
Selfish, self-contained, stupid,
Like fans running on the pitch,
Jumping on each other after a 90th-minute winner.
Like leaving someone out when you are playing a game.
I feel scared that these people actually exist.
Like walking home in the dark when your house is far away.
Troublemakers,
They cause misery to too many people's lives.

Camryn Williams (11)
St Luke's Halsall CE Primary School, Liverpool

Are They Real 'Mates'?

Are they real *mates*?
Do they force you to do things you don't like?
Forceful, intimidating, scary.
Like being out of control on a roller-coaster ride.
Like parachuting out of a plane for the first time.
It makes me feel disgusted.
Like being let down by the people you know.
Are they real *mates*?
Gang members aren't *mates*.

Lucy Ainscough (11)
St Luke's Halsall CE Primary School, Liverpool

Secrets Will Be Found

Secrets will be found,
By the police or that person you call *mate*.
Pointless, ridiculous, worthless.
Like trying to hide the chocolate you stole.
Like someone finding out something you didn't
want them to know.
It makes me confused,
Like when I get shouted at for no reason.
Secrets will be found,
Will you make the right choice?

Lily-Mae Cureton (10)
St Luke's Halsall CE Primary School, Liverpool

Be Brave And Confident

Be brave and confident,
That is what you need to be.
Inspirer, idol, icon.
Like being a hand that pulls a child
Back from a dangerous, busy road.
Like being Superman who can reverse time.
It makes me feel ready.
Like waiting for a whistle's blow to start a race.
Be brave and confident,
For it saves a life and makes a community safer.

Grace Critchley (11)
St Luke's Halsall CE Primary School, Liverpool

Prison

Prison,
Somewhere you don't want to end up.
Disturbing, frightening, shameful.
Like being locked away from family and friends forever.
Like not being loved on Valentine's Day.
Starting to feel sorry for yourself.
Like being stranded on a desert island never to be rescued.
Prison,
Don't have regrets, think before you do.

Nathan Hughes (11)
St Luke's Halsall CE Primary School, Liverpool

Gangs

Gangs,
When you get in, you can't get out.
Dangerous, deadly and intimidating.
As dangerous as going to space unprepared.
As hard to speak out as a person telling the truth.
It's a situation that needs to be dealt with all over
the world.
As deadly as a lion stalking its prey.
Gangs,
Once you get in, you can't get out!

Austin Williams (11)
St Luke's Halsall CE Primary School, Liverpool

Taking A Life

Taking a life,
Will change their loved ones forever.
Stupid, idiotic, unforgettable.
Like taking your most precious belongings away.
Like memories are the only thing left.
It makes me feel heartbroken for families.
Like all their hopes drifting away.
Taking a life,
Reminds us the world isn't perfect.

Grace Dawson (10)
St Luke's Halsall CE Primary School, Liverpool

Revenge

Revenge,
What everyone wants.
Stupid, sly, selfish.
Like a thing you need to do tingling constantly
At the back of your mind.
Like a cunning fox catching his prey,
I feel threated.
Like being in a small, dark room filled with
An unfamiliar face.
Revenge,
Think, don't retaliate.

Lilly Rose McParlan (11)
St Luke's Halsall CE Primary School, Liverpool

The Plastic Problem

The plastic problem
Started 500 years ago.
Critical, colossal, consistent.
Like the huge fires in Australia.
Like a tornado rapidly whizzing around 1,000 miles per hour.
It makes me feel devastated and upset.
Like killing an animal for no reason.
The plastic problem,
Reuse, reduce, recycle.

Amy Martin (11)
St Luke's Halsall CE Primary School, Liverpool

The Time Wasters

The time wasters
Forever doing something stupid
Dumb, dangerous, disturbing
Like a way that is not supposed to happen
Like the Joker killing Batman
It makes me feel unsafe
Like people being trapped in a concentration camp
The time wasters
Reminding us that the world will never be peaceful.

Robyn Cunningham (10)
St Luke's Halsall CE Primary School, Liverpool

Losing An Innocent Life

Losing an innocent life,
Affecting a family forever.
Horrifying, hazardous, heartbreaking.
Like walking into an empty, dark world.
Like having your own life taken away.
I feel intimidated and scared.
Like living in an abandoned island.
Losing an innocent life,
A path you never want to go down.

Vinu Wewalwala (11)
St Luke's Halsall CE Primary School, Liverpool

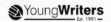

Getting Your Own Back!

Getting your own back!
It is not exciting.
Daft, dangerous, dreadful.
Like swimming in a sea surrounded by sharks.
Like finding out something heartbreaking.
It makes me feel vulnerable.
Like a cat pouncing on a mouse.
Getting your own back!
Reminds us how they take the lives of innocent people.

Isaac Moran (10)
St Luke's Halsall CE Primary School, Liverpool

Hiding Secrets

Hiding secrets.
A jail cell awaits.
Stupid, suspicious, senseless,
You are as guilty as the person who did it.
Like someone making every mistake.
It makes me feel worried.
Like someone stalking you in the dead of night.
Hiding secrets,
Don't be afraid to tell the truth.

Connor Dwyer (11)
St Luke's Halsall CE Primary School, Liverpool

Hell On Earth

Hell on Earth,
Tears a family apart.
Dangerous, devastation, disturbing.
Like ripping your heart out and feeding it to a lion.
Like selling your soul to the Devil.
It makes me feel distraught.
Like losing a loved one.
Hell on Earth,
Your life will never be the same again.

Shay Gorman (10)
St Luke's Halsall CE Primary School, Liverpool

The Dark-Hooded Man

The dark-hooded man,
A waste of our time.
Dangerous, shameful, pointless.
Like a hurricane in your mind.
Like a nightmare coming to life.
It makes me feel frightened and panicked,
Like a penguin in an ocean of sharks.
The dark-hooded man,
The shadow of the world.

Ava Hargreaves (10)
St Luke's Halsall CE Primary School, Liverpool

Criminal Citizens

Criminal citizens,
Out for revenge.
Self-centred, selfish, stupid.
Like your best friend betraying you by finding a
new friend.
Like scoring only one in a test.
It makes me feel angry.
Like parents losing their only child.
Criminal citizens,
Why are they doing it?

Lyla Durdey (10)
St Luke's Halsall CE Primary School, Liverpool

Gangs And Bangs

Gangs and bangs,
Putting many families at risk.
Scary, sacrificing, frightening.
Like losing your only child.
As frightening as standing alone in the trenches.
They make me feel unsafe.
Like being chased by a clown.
Gangs and bangs,
Get away and get safe.

Sienna Nugent (11)
St Luke's Halsall CE Primary School, Liverpool

Weapons

Weapons,
Ending so many lives.
Idiotic, demoralising, depressing.
Like a lion snatching its prey.
Like holding something that can change a family.
It is absolute stupidity.
Like stealing something but you know it's wrong to do it.
Weapons,
Stay safe and clear.

Edward Fell (11)
St Luke's Halsall CE Primary School, Liverpool

Gang Mates

Gang mates,
They are never your mates,
Dangerous, daring, disturbing,
Like never being able to see your family again.
Like you were about to be killed.
It makes me feel terrified,
Like a rabbit caught in headlights.
Gang mates,
Get away and stay safe.

Rose Gartland (10)
St Luke's Halsall CE Primary School, Liverpool

Cold-Blooded Gangs

Cold-blooded gangs.
A sad excuse of a lifestyle.
Dangerous, dark, devious.
Like robbers of peace.
Like someone who only likes to torment.
It makes me feel scared.
Like a sheep surrounded by wolves.
Cold-blooded gangs,
The shadow of regret.

Lizzie Smith (11)
St Luke's Halsall CE Primary School, Liverpool

Retaliation

Retaliation,
Don't want to get involved.
Shameful, wrong, terrible.
Like being stung by a swarm of bees.
I feel it is a terrible thing.
Like being told off for something you didn't do.
Retaliation,
Don't hit back!

Jessica Dearden (10)
St Luke's Halsall CE Primary School, Liverpool

Threats And Regrets

Threats and regrets,
They put your family in danger.
Dangerous, dumb, devastating.
Like a gang will attack me.
Like a gang will kill me.
Like a rabbit being chased by a fox.
Threats and regrets,
Get away and get safe.

Tom Windsor (11)
St Luke's Halsall CE Primary School, Liverpool

Criminals

Criminals,
A menace in our community.
Dangerous, powerful, cruel.
Like a cat tormenting a mouse.
Like friends not telling the truth.
It makes me feel angry and scared.
Criminals,
See them, report them, stop them!

Jamie Aldridge (11)
St Luke's Halsall CE Primary School, Liverpool

Did I See An Alien?

I was going on an adventure with my latest
invention,
I should have been in school so I could get
detention.
I was going on my flying chair,
I could even lose a little bit of hair.

Five, four, three, two, one,
Whoosh! I was off into space!

I saw all the planets and even the moon
What was that noise? That really loud boom?
I thought it was coming from nearby Mars,
But I couldn't see anything from this far

As I got closer, I saw something odd,
He introduced himself as an alien called Todd.
He had four rounded eyes, five stubby arms,
At this point in time, I tried to stay calm.
He had two mushroom heads,
A body green and blue,
Some Shrek-like ears,
What should I do?

He showed me around his secret world,
I noticed a sign that said *No Girls!*
But I kept on following and guess what I saw?
An underground aquarium and so much more!
A crocodile with no teeth,
A shark with no fin,
A piranha with a great big smile,
A whale that was really thin.

I loved my time here in space,
I loved trying my invention!
Back down to Earth I needed to go,
Ready for my detention!

Jessica Pendegrass (9)
St Mary's CE Primary School, Chiddingfold

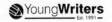

If I Were An Astronaut

If I were an astronaut,
I'd fly away to space,
In my little shining rocket,
To a dark and empty place

I'd circle around Venus,
I'd touch the Milky Way,
I'd walk the moon, I'd swim the stars
Then I would go and play.

With all the families of aliens,
Two heads, four eyes, three noses,
And when I say, "I need to go."
They would hand me some mouldy roses.

It all reminded me of chocolate,
Galaxy, Milky Way, Mars bars,
But my favourite bit would have to be,
Seeing the shimmering stars.

On my spectacular journey,
I saw, I played, I learned.

But when I stepped on Mars,
It was obvious my feet were burned.

I thought I'd go for a spin on Saturn,
And slide upon its rings,
But then it got quite boring
And I thought of other things.

Like smelling Uranus,
Going close to the sun,
Seeing Jupiter's red spot,
That sounds like so much fun!

Then I look at my green and blue home,
I want to go back, but how? I'm alone.
This is the end of my little dream,
Good luck in space, for I have come and been.

Amber Talman

St Mary's CE Primary School, Chiddingfold

A Starry Night At Midnight

All the stars, one by one,
Made their way up the stairs,
As the sun and blue skies above, tucked in their chairs.
All the stars took their final bow,
Said goodnight and walked off saying ciao.
As all the stars reached their final step,
Some of them even wept.
Then the sun and blue sky stood up tall and proudly.
All of a sudden, the sun yawned very loudly.
I'm a star, I love my job.
I hate it when I look down and see an angry mob.
My favourite bit of the day,
Is when NASA rockets fly past.
It reminds me that when you're having fun,
Time flies fast.
Five, four, three, two, one, it makes me jump.
When a star falls out of the sky it makes a thump.

I'm a shining star,
I hate that beeping noise made by cars.
I'm close to space,
Although it's a dark, empty place.
I live around Jupiter,
There are a lot of aliens that grow stupider.
One day, I hope to live around the sun,
That would be fun.
Now you have heard my story,
Little did you know my best friend is called Corey,
That's just a fact,
I'll be back!

Mattie Thompson
St Mary's CE Primary School, Chiddingfold

Aliens Are Invading

People of Earth love space,
Jupiter, Saturn and Mars.
They really love the night sky,
With its bright, shining stars.
So when we came, it was a delight,
But we gave some people quite a fright.

We arrived on Earth in our spaceships and all,
Round the corner to invade the mall.
We scooted past the park as quick as we can,
We didn't want to wake any man.
Into the cafe for a quick pit stop,
We were messy, so get ready with the mop.
We're all really strange looking,
But we all love one thing.
We all have three googly eyes and more.
But we have one secret: we can stare straight into
the Earth's core!

Venus, Saturn and Neptune too,
We love our home but we love yours too.
We're aliens, why wouldn't we?

We love your tall buildings and blue seas.
We love your pretty flowers,
And the buzzing bees.
So that's why we came to see your land,
And your little bugs and hot sand.
But after that invasion, I think us aliens will be banned!

Florence Spicer (10)
St Mary's CE Primary School, Chiddingfold

Rocket Man

When I am older, I will travel up to space,
Entering the galaxy with a smile on my face.
Next I will rip into the Milky Way,
Then land on Venus, what a special day!

Venus is without a doubt,
The hottest of them all.
I've learnt lots about this planet,
A burning red fireball.

I also want to go to the moon,
Just like my dad, Neil, did.
You'll probably know him, our surname's
Armstrong.
That's right, I'm his kid.

I will jump in my suit made of titanium,
It will be strong and silver, just like aluminium.
I will find an alien soon, just you wait and see,
I would like my rocket to be as red as red can be.

The location of my toilet worries me a bit,
I can't help but wonder where on Earth I'll sit.

I might feel claustrophobic after a day or two,
But if my dad can do it, then I can do it too.

Joseph Mercer (9)
St Mary's CE Primary School, Chiddingfold

My Big Adventure

I step into the rocket, I look at the seat,
A little bit nervous, I can feel my heart beat.
I walk to the window and feel myself glow,
Finally, a few preparations before I go!

Whoosh! And off the rocket goes,
I fall with a thump and bash my nose.
I run to the chair and strap myself in,
I know my journey is about to begin.

As my rocket is high off the ground,
I look out the window and look all around.
As I get higher and arrive in space,
You should see the look on my face.

Mars is bumpy and hot on the top,
I like this planet, I like it a lot.
It's the fourth from the sun and ruby red,
I imagined it like this when I've been lying in bed.

My adventure is over, it's come to an end,
I'm excited to tell all my friends.

So now it's time to return back home,
Because I am fed up of being all alone.

Lily Sabi Parry (9)
St Mary's CE Primary School, Chiddingfold

A Dream In Space

My helmet is misting up,
From the air of my breath.
Earth down below,
Pluto up ahead.
Aliens in saucers,
The moon shining bright,
Is this a dream in the middle of the night?
I see a shooting star whistle over my head,
I make a wish not to wake up in bed.
My mum would never let me go to space,
So this is my chance to put on my brave face.
I'll visit the moon,
Tumble and turn,
Maybe meet an alien,
I wonder what I'll learn.
The moon is a pearl,
At the bottom of the sea.
I've never met an alien,
But that doesn't bother me.
So I zoom in my rocket,

Back to bed,
Where I think of the journey that lies ahead.
I could meet an alien,
For the very first time,
Maybe see Jupiter
With my very own eyes.
But right now it's time for bed,
So I'm going to snuggle up with Astronaut Ted.

Lila Cooke (9)
St Mary's CE Primary School, Chiddingfold

Alien Invasion

I long to see Mercury, I long to see Mars,
But if only I could be like Captain Frars.
He can definitely swoop and he can sway,
No wonder he gets paid twice a day!
Why am I in mission control?
I can soar, I can jump,
Though it left me with quite a lump.
But wait, what's that?
Is it a cat?
It's there on my screen, haven't you seen?
It has two heads, three eyes and a body twice the size.

"It's an alien," says the voice behind me.
"But how on Earth did it find me?"
I turn around only to see,
"Argh! An alien!"
The voice replies with a sloppy sound,
"Yep, that's me!"
A black hole appears in the ground.

I fall and I fall,
I am bound to be drowned.
But I fall right into my cosy bed,
All cuddled up with Mr Ted.
Maybe next time instead.

Bea Monk (9)
St Mary's CE Primary School, Chiddingfold

Black World

The space was full of stars.
We could hear the songs from Planet Mars,
The fourth planet in line from the sun.
We get in our rocket, zooming into space.
We saw the Milky Way,
Shooting stars, the galaxy and the empty space.
We passed all eight planets,
Venus, Earth, Mars, Jupiter, Saturn, Uranus,
Neptune the windiest planet.
We went past the moon,
Hearing *The Clangers* clanging.
We saw the scary black hole,
We nearly got caught.

The first time I went into space,
I was very scared, but now I love it.
The galaxy looks like chocolate,
I wanted to get out and have some,
But I knew it wasn't real.
Soon we were heading back home,
Back past Neptune, Uranus, Saturn,
Jupiter, Mars, Venus and Mercury.

We landed at home all tired, ready for bed,
Ready for the next flight to space.

Owen Wilson (9)
St Mary's CE Primary School, Chiddingfold

Space

Space is such an empty place,
Meteoroids that are quick like rockets and ships.
I had always wanted to go to Mars,
And look at the wonderful shooting stars.
I also hoped I could fly,
But to do this, I needed to be launched into the sky!

As the countdown echoed around,
I heard a very deafening sound.
The engines started and the floor and the rocket parted.
Up I went into the darkness,
There I was in space, a quite lifeless place.
First I started at Mars,
And then I swam through all the stars.
Then I made my way to Jupiter,
There I found people that were a lot stupider.

Whilst we went back down,
I was sad and had a frown.
Then I said goodbye.

When I got home,
I was all alone,
Thinking about my trip.

Noah McCarthy-Holland (9)
St Mary's CE Primary School, Chiddingfold

Space!

Space is a place without a human race.
Black holes, galaxies, Milky Ways and more.
Space is a place with aliens and stars, craters and moons,
There's a lot more to explore.
This is amazing, with planets and meteoroids,
But here's some ups and downs, like no civilisation and towns.
Space is a place with bright things and the sun,
But it's also weird, with a bit of fun.

Aliens might live there, who knows,
'It's their home' the saying goes.
Back on Earth, there's gravity and trees,
In space, there's none of these.
In space, there might be a place where animals roam,
Get your passport because they're probably in Rome.
This space is a wonderful place,
If you want a visit, you have to bring your case.

Edward Seymour

St Mary's CE Primary School, Chiddingfold

The Slimy Alien

The rocket zoomed into space as I was in the main
cockpit,
I landed on Jupiter.
It was freezing, I saw a flying saucer,
It was going to land on Jupiter too!
The saucer landed and inside were aliens.
The aliens were so slimy, they all had three eyes,
They had golden armour on their slimy bodies.
The aliens took me to their ship,
I was frightened!
The ship had a giant power crystal,
It could work any electronic things,
And gave the aliens superpowers.
I managed to knock out one of the aliens,
I stole the keys and got out of jail.
I threw a bomb at the crystal,
The ship crashed back on Jupiter,
So I used my ship to escape.
Back on Earth...
The aliens were never to be seen again!

Isaac Lee-Smith (10)
St Mary's CE Primary School, Chiddingfold

There Is An Alien Under My Bed

When I said goodnight
To my parents that night,
I saw something spectacular,
A thing with no good manner.
It was running under my bed, going a bit red.
What could it be? I went to see.

It was as big as my finger,
As straight as a pillar.
He had four eyes as small as crumbs,
If that's not weird, he had six thumbs!

He climbed onto my shoulder,
And was as heavy as a boulder.
He ripped down my painting,
And then started skating.

But then he spoke,
He said his spaceship had broke.
It had lost a wheel, so I put it back on,
And all of a sudden, a blue light switched on.

He got ready,
He got set,
Then *whoosh!* he went,
And I never saw my alien again.

Camille Freeman Lecerf (9)
St Mary's CE Primary School, Chiddingfold

Alone In Space

One moment I'm saying goodbye,
The next, I'm in a rocket, flying through the sky.
All on my own in the blackness,
Am I alone here in the unknown?
So far from home.
Up here I miss it all,
Civilisation and all.

Up in the black beast's belly,
In space, there is no up, down, left, or right.
The ground team gives me directions,
Save me from the humming black known as space.
Wait, what was that?
A bang at the back of the ship?
Help me! Save me!
What do I do?
I've been up here five days,
Save me, please.

What is that coming out of the black?
Another ship coming to save me.

One moment I was in space,
The next I'm back home.

Findlay Price

St Mary's CE Primary School, Chiddingfold

The Aliens Who Attacked Me

Three, two, one... blast-off!
Round Jupiter, under Saturn,
Over Uranus, brake! We're at Neptune,
Oh, I just blew off the engine.

Now I am stuck in space,
What can I do?
Oh, a flying saucer,
Maybe they can help me
Oh, I just called aliens! Argh!

I really need to get that engine going,
Or the aliens will kill me.
I hope I don't run all around Neptune,
Because I will be here for days.

I come across an old jetpack,
I fly around Neptune, across to Jupiter.
I stop at Pluto, where there are even more aliens.
The other aliens jump at me,
But I manage to get away.

I fly back to Earth,
That was my adventure day.

Jasmine Rollings
St Mary's CE Primary School, Chiddingfold

The Aliens That Invited Me To Tea

I saw an alien simply grass green,
An interesting fact, he loved green tea.
I saw his eyes, they were violet purple,
He liked to bathe in his very own whirlpool.
Four eyes he had and a lumpy blue forehead.
He did not have a house or a naughty pet mouse.

Then he read a copy of the latest alien stuff,
Meanwhile I dreamed of my bed of puff.
But I could not be rude and say he was boring,
Anyway, in England, it would be pouring.
Then we had a party,
And next, I set up a class of pilates.

Tonight was full of fright,
And I would not forget the sight
Of my space friend.
Just maybe, aliens are not so boring,
After all, just maybe.

Evelyn Harrison (9)
St Mary's CE Primary School, Chiddingfold

Off Into Space!

I was sitting in the cockpit, countdown just begun,
Engine roaring, rocket rumbling and off into space.
First past Mars, then past Jupiter, and Saturn is
where I did land.
I got up and went outside. *Wow! Loads of aliens!*

Yes, aliens. Big aliens. Purple aliens. Very happy
aliens.
Their arms were super long, wiggling everywhere.
A big purple head, with no body at all, it also had
no legs either,
Aliens rolling here to there.

I went to talk to one, I could not understand it,
But I knew it was friendly because it was cheerful.
I took it home, back to Earth, where it was nice
and warm.
Soon I had to let him go, back to his family in
space.

Ben Church (9)
St Mary's CE Primary School, Chiddingfold

My Alien Friend

Once I met an alien, he came from outer space,
He had two eyes, a knobbly head and a weird-looking face.
He had greenish skin and two peg legs,
But had two UFOs that looked like boiled eggs.
He didn't make any friends,
Because he drove people around the bends.
Apart from me, his best mate,
He lent me a spaceship and left it at the gate.
We met on the moon and landed with a crack,
To Mars and Jupiter, and all the way back.
Using lasers to clear the way,
So that it didn't ruin our day.
He dropped me off at home,
And knocked over my garden gnome.
As I waved him goodbye,
It got me quite sad and made me cry.

Samuel Ponting (10)
St Mary's CE Primary School, Chiddingfold

The Universe

The universe is an infinite place that doesn't have a start or end,
The universe is a mysterious place which has surprises around every bend.
The universe is a place with galaxies, planets and stars,
The universe is a place where there might be life on Mars.
The universe is a place with no air or gravity,
The universe is a place of endless possibility.
The universe is a place where unexpected things can happen,
The universe is a place which holds the planet Saturn.
The universe is a place filled with wonder and awe,
The universe is a place bursting with so much more.

Barnaby Harrall (9)
St Mary's CE Primary School, Chiddingfold

My Rocket And Me

I step into my rocket,
I look outside,
With a touch of glow, makes me shine,
Three... two... one... blast-off!

I go to Saturn that has a ring of rocks,
And the smell of Uranus makes me cough,
Found on Saturn lies an ox,
But the weird thing is he wears woolly socks.

I wonder where to go next,
Then I quickly find a nearby nest,
I quickly put it to the test,
To go on an adventure, a simple quest.

I go to Neptune,
On the 14th June,
And in the distance there are floating balloons,
With my naked eye, I see the hundreds of moons.

Jessica Dawes (10)
St Mary's CE Primary School, Chiddingfold

Space Poem!

Three, two, one... blast-off!
Out into space, really far away,
I've been staring at the darkness for most of the
day.
I can see all the planets and most of the stars,
Mercury, Venus, Earth and Mars.
Jupiter is enormous, just like a big brother,
Saturn's winds are faster than others.
Uranus is covered in water, a huge monsoon,
Neptune is many shades of blue and shaped like a
balloon.
I've passed all eight planets, eight of them in a
row,
There used to a ninth whose name was Pluto.

But I'm done for now,
So goodbye for now!

Toby Bennett (9)
St Mary's CE Primary School, Chiddingfold

The Planets And Me!

What was that thing coming towards me?
Argh! What was it? It was getting bigger and
bigger.
As I passed Mercury and Venus, I saw little green
figures.
The metal object turned left to Mars.
As I passed Jupiter, I saw a big storm swirling.
As I passed Saturn, I saw the big ring spinning.
As I passed Uranus, I smelt a weird smell.
It was the smell of rotten eggs.
As I passed Neptune, it blew my rocket back to
Earth!
The metal object landed in Perth!

Max Cansfield (9)
St Mary's CE Primary School, Chiddingfold